"BEHAVE IN PUBLIC!"

CREDITS

Producer
 Ron Berry

Editor
 Orly Kelly

What to do when your mom or dad says... "BEHAVE IN PUBLIC!"

By
JOY BERRY

GROLIER ENTERPRISES CORP.

Has your mother or father ever told you to . . .

When your mom or dad tells you to behave in public, do you wonder . . .

If any of this sounds familiar to you, you're going to **love** this book.

Because this book is going to tell you exactly how to behave in public.

BOARDING A VEHICLE

You can be gracious whenever you board a car, bus, train, or airplane by doing these things:

1. Be on time for the departure so that you will not keep anyone waiting.

2. Let the people who are already in the vehicle get out before you get in.

3. Do not crowd or push your way into a vehicle. Wait your turn patiently.

4. Have your money or ticket ready so that you will not cause the people behind you to wait.

FINDING YOUR SEAT IN A VEHICLE

After you have boarded a car, bus, train, or airplane, you can be gracious by doing these things:

1. If you have been assigned a seat, sit in it without complaining.
2. If you have not been assigned a seat, sit in the first available one.
3. If you have baggage or packages, keep them to yourself under your seat or on your lap. Do not take up additional space with them.
4. If someone else needs your seat more than you do, be kind and give it up. If you must stand, hold onto something so that you will not fall or bump into anyone.

RIDING IN A VEHICLE

You can be gracious when you ride in a vehicle by
doing these things:

1. Do not bother anyone around you by talking
   too loudly.
2. Do not do other rude things like reading over a
   person's shoulder.

3. Converse with the person next to you only if talk is encouraged.

4. Do not expect the person sitting next to you to entertain you.

5. Do not leave any trash or litter behind you.

6. If you are in an inside seat, excuse yourself when you are ready to leave, and avoid bumping into the person or stepping on toes.

7. Excuse yourself if you need to make your way through a crowd to the door, and avoid bumping into people or stepping on their feet as you go.

8. Leave the vehicle as soon as possible after it has come to a complete stop so that you will not detain the passengers who wish to board.

Entertaining Yourself While Riding in a Vehicle

If you want to make sure that your journey is not a boring one, take something along to do while you are riding. Here are a few suggestions:

1. Take something along to do, like pencils and paper for drawing or writing.
2. Take something along to play, like a deck of cards, a game, or some puzzles.

3. Take something along to read, like a book or magazine.

4. Take something along to listen to, like a tape recorder or radio. (Do this *only* if your radio or tape recorder has an earphone, so that you won't impose what you are listening to on the passengers around you.)

RIDING AN ELEVATOR

You can be gracious whenever you ride an elevator by doing these things:

1. Give the people who are leaving the elevator a chance to get out before you get in.
2. If an elevator is crowded, don't squeeze your way in. Instead, wait for it to come back to you or take another one.

3. Unless there is an elevator attendant to do it for you, push the button for the floor you want as you enter the elevator. If you can't get to the button, kindly ask someone standing near the button to push it for you.

4. If you will be riding in the elevator for some time (because there are several stops ahead of you), step to the back of the elevator so that you will not stand in the way of people needing to get out before you.

5. If you will be getting off the elevator soon, stay to the front of the elevator (but step to one side, if possible) so that you will not have to push through everyone to get out.

6. Do not push and shove your way out of an elevator. Instead, say something like, "Excuse me, may I get out?" or "Out, please," so that people in front of you can move out of your way.

RIDING AN ESCALATOR

Whenever you ride an escalator or a moving ramp, you can be gracious by doing these things:

1. Wait your turn to get on the escalator or ramp.
2. Do not stand too close to the person who has stepped onto the escalator right before you. Allow a few spaces to pass before you step on.

3. If you are not in a hurry and want to stand still on the escalator, stand to your far right so that people may pass you on your left. Also, make sure you do not block someone who wants to pass you.

4. If you are in a hurry and want to walk on the escalator, carefully pass the person in front of you on the left side and say "Excuse me" as you pass.

ATTENDING A PERFORMANCE

You can be gracious when you go to a performance by doing these things:

1. Bring only those things that are absolutely necessary (like a purse or wallet), so that you will not take up unnecessary space in and around your seat with your possessions.

2. Be on time for the performance so that you will not cause a disturbance by coming in late.

TAP
TAP
TAP

3. Let the people who were at the preceding performance out of the theater before you go in.

4. Do not crowd or push your way into the theater. Wait your turn patiently.

5. Have your money or ticket ready so that you will not cause the people behind you to wait.

6. Go to the rest room or get your refreshments before you sit down and during intermission so that you will not have to get up during the performance.

Arriving After a Performance Begins

Once the performance begins, you can be gracious by doing these things:

1. If you arrive after the performance has begun, wait for the usher to seat you.
2. If there is no usher to seat you, wait for your eyes to adjust to the dark and then quickly and quietly find your seat.

3. If you have been assigned a seat, sit in it without complaining.

4. If you must pass in front of others to get to your seat, face the stage or screen while you are passing them. Try not to bump people or to step on their toes.

   Do not say anything unless you accidentally bump into someone or step on someone's toes. If you do this, say "Excuse me" very softly.

Watching a Performance

As you watch the performance, you can be gracious by doing these things:

1. Do not bother anyone around you by whispering, talking loudly, or doing other rude things like humming, whistling, snapping gum, or tapping or kicking the seats in front of you.

2. If eating during the performance is permitted, do so neatly and privately.

3. If someone needs to pass in front of you to get to a seat, pull your legs in or stand up so that the person can get by easily. If the person says, "Excuse me," you may want to say, "Surely."

4. If you find that you do not like a live performance, do your best to wait it out until intermission or the end of the performance. Try not to leave in the middle.

5. Avoid criticizing the performance while it is taking place. Wait for intermission, or preferably until after you have left the theater.

6. You should show your appreciation for the performance by applauding at the appropriate times.

7. Do not begin to put your things on or to leave the theater before the performance is over.

8. When you leave, do not leave any trash or litter behind you. Always clean up after yourself.

ATTENDING ATHLETIC EVENTS

Many of the rules that apply to the theater also apply to athletic events.

When you attend an athletic event, you should show the same sensitivity and kindness you would show at a theater performance.

VISITING A CHURCH

In regard to another person's religion, you can be
gracious by doing these things:

1. Never criticize or make fun of another person's
   religion.

2. Ask questions about a person's religion only if you are genuinely interested.

Whenever you visit a church, you can be gracious by doing these things:

1. Before you visit a church, find out ahead of time whether there is any special way you should dress, and then dress accordingly. For example, some churches will require that you cover your head and/or arms.

2. Find out ahead of time what is going to take place during the service so that you will know when you should and should not participate. For example, some churches will not want you to participate in communion if you are not a member of the church. In other churches, it won't matter whether or not you are a member.

3. It is not necessary for you to do everything the church members are doing, but you may feel more comfortable if you stand when they stand, sit when they sit, or kneel when they kneel.

4. During the service, it is extremely important that you be respectful. Sit quietly and pay attention as much as possible to what is going on.

GOING SHOPPING

Whenever you go shopping, you can be gracious
by doing these things:

1. When a salesperson says something like, "May I
   help you?" answer something like, "Yes please" (if
   you want help), or "No, thank you, I would prefer
   to look for awhile" (if you do not want help).

2. Do not interrupt a salesperson who is helping another person. Wait your turn to be helped.

3. Do not complain to sales people about prices. They have nothing to do with them.

4. Do not handle merchandise you do not intend to buy.

5. Handle all merchandise carefully.

6. If you break or damage something, call it to a salesperson's attention and offer to pay for it.

7. If you try on clothes, put them back on hangers afterwards. Do not leave them on the dressing room floor.

8. Do not use anything you plan to return, and return it as soon as possible.

Remember, whenever you are out in public, it is important to treat everyone around you the way you would want to be treated. If you do this, you will be sure to do the right thing.

THE END of not knowing how to behave in public.